TOOLS FOR TEACHERS

- **ATOS:** 0.8
- **GRL:** C
- **LEXILE:** 160L
- **CURRICULUM CONNECTIONS:** animals
- **WORD COUNT:** 101

Skills to Teach

- **HIGH-FREQUENCY WORDS:** are, at, can, do, has, he, her, him, his, it, look, no, see, she, the, they, to, you
- **CONTENT WORDS:** ears, eyes, calf, cow, horns, milk, mouth, pattern, spots, tail
- **PUNCTUATION:** periods, question marks, comma, exclamation point
- **WORD STUDY:** silent *l* (*calf*); /z/, spelled *s* (*ears*, *eyes*, *flies*); *r*-controlled vowels (*hear*, *horns*, *mother*, *pattern*, *turn*); long /a/, spelled *ai* (*tail*), *a_e* (*safe*); long /i/, spelled *eye* (*eyes*), *ie* (*flies*)
- **TEXT TYPE:** information report

Before Reading Activities

- Read the title and give a simple statement of the main idea.
- Have students "walk" though the book and talk about what they see in the pictures.
- Introduce new vocabulary by having students predict the first letter and locate the word in the text.
- Discuss any unfamiliar concepts that are in the text.

After Reading Activities

List the different parts of a calf, such as eyes, ears, horns, and tail, on the board and consider which farm babies (lambs, foals, chicks, etc.) might have the same parts, and if so, how they are similar or different. Does a chick have a tail? How about a lamb? Following the children's suggestions, write the animal's name underneath the body part and discuss the appropriateness of each match.

Tadpole Books are published by Jump!, 5357 Penn Avenue South, Minneapolis, MN 55419, www.jumplibrary.com

Copyright ©2018 Jump. International copyright reserved in all countries. No part of this book may be reproduced in any form without written permission from the publisher.

Editor: Jenny Fretland VanVoorst   **Designer:** Anna Peterson

Photo Credits: Getty: Jmichl, cover. Shutterstock: Eric Isselee, 1; Dudarev Mikhail, 2–3; Zeljko Radojko, 4–5; khanongjansri, 6–7; smereka, 8–9, 10–11; Radek Sturgolewski, 12–13; Bildagentur Zoonar GmbH, 14–15.

Library of Congress Cataloging-in-Publication Data
Names: Mayerling, Tim, author.
Title: Calves / by Tim Mayerling.
Description: Minneapolis: Jump!, Inc., 2017. | Series: Farm babies | Includes index. | Audience: Ages 3 to 6.
Identifiers: LCCN 2017019215 (print) | LCCN 2017018071 (ebook) | ISBN 9781624966132 (ebook) | ISBN 9781620317662 (hardcover: alk. paper) | ISBN 9781620317860 (pbk.)
Subjects: LCSH: Calves—Juvenile literature.
Classification: LCC SF197.5 (print) | LCC SF197.5 .M328 2017 (ebook) | DDC 636/.07—dc23
LC record available at https://lccn.loc.gov/2017019215

FARM BABIES

CALVES

by Tim Mayerling

TABLE OF CONTENTS

Calves 2

Words to Know 16

Index 16

tadpole
books

CALVES

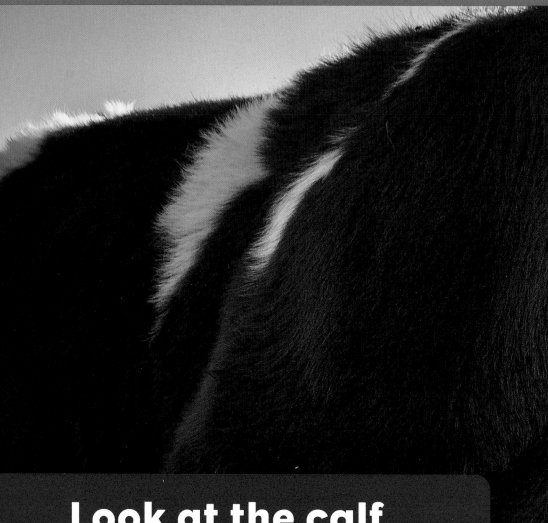

Look at the calf. Do you see his eyes?

They are big and brown.

**Look at the calf.
Do you see her spots?**

No other cow has the same pattern.

**Look at the calf.
Do you see his ears?**

ear

He can turn them to hear.

**Look at the calf.
Do you see her tail?**

tail

It keeps
away flies.

horn

**Look at the calf.
Do you see his horns?**

They help keep him safe.

**Look at the calf.
Do you see her mouth?**

She drinks milk
from her mother.

Look at the calf. Do you see her?

The calf sees you, too!

WORDS TO KNOW

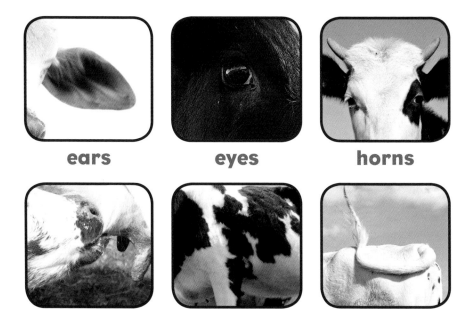

ears   eyes   horns

mouth   spots   tail

INDEX

ears 6

eyes 2

horns 10

milk 13

mother 13

mouth 12

pattern 5

safe 11

spots 4

tail 8